INSIDE THE ORB OF AN ORACLE

DANNIE RUTH

C&R Press
Conscious & Responsible

All Rights Reserved

Printed in the United States of America

First Edition
1 2 3 4 5 6 7 8 9

Selections of up to two pages may be reproduced without permission. To reproduce more than two pages of any one portion of this book write to C&R Press publishers John Gosslee and Andrew Sullivan.

Cover art by Nate Lewis
Interior design by Jojo Rita

Copyright ©2020 Dannie Ruth

ISBN: 978-1-949540-16-1

C&R Press
Conscious & Responsible
crpress.org

For special discounted bulk purchases, please contact:
C&R Press sales@crpress.org
Contact info@crpress.org to book events, readings and author signings.

DEDICATION

to Creator for this gift,
to my ancestors for treasured memories,
to my abundant family for transcendental love,
to the soil we are rooted, to the native and to the stolen,
to change, to grief, to peace with uncertainty,
to my master teachers and to my keen students
to universal language, to color, to shape, to rhythm
to me for creating this and to you for arriving

INSIDE THE ORB OF AN ORACLE

the sphere

It is Monday. I arrive smooth like horns on the *Outkast* chorus.
I am neon light blending in ensemble with a thriving trio.
My father hums hymns of hope, while chords and strings stretch
across my mother's belly as if sheet music has been delicately plastered
onto a globe, guiding my sister's hands across rhythms and rhymes
she, the first divine child granted me two names.
I, the end and the beginning of the whole
the fourth corner, the final right angle

our double dynamic duo complete: *just the four of us*
we can make it if we try, just the four of us, the three of you

and I was born on a Monday, many years ago today
like my ancestors, transitioning trios into quartets
aligning right with left, lathered in equilibrium
balancing both sides of the car, the dinner table, the photograph

the sphere: separated equally and equitably into four
three dimensional pieces that create a world extending to all we touch.

Roots

food family music intersects
(as told by my uncle Reggie)

amen.
romaine lettuce topped with avocado tri pepper spread and croutons. lump crab meat optional. kale and collard greens, vegetable soup with shrimp brown rice noodles. grilled shrimp infused with avocado essence and steamed mussels with tequila essence. then this here is that soufeast Thai remix (had to add the pasta sauce it was a little dry). oh, my goodness. I'm eating oxtails. finally, I beat Bobby Flay!
as a school teacher extraordinaire, let's stay away from 'dope'. let's say excellent. do not fuck with dope or drugs. fruits vegetables and love for family and friends will give you all the sustained foundation needed. I hope you take time to cook for yourself. let's do a family cookbook. Reach out to Raheem, I'm sure he has a recipe
eat moor raw
photograph I always dream of
being as extraordinary as Gordon Parks, my photos will capture copper people, copper colored people, captive copper colored people protect your mind body and soul. protect you. study study study and then study some moor. we are parents of this universe. teach respectfully. read. explore. enjoy you. with love. please call your grandparents and get your questions
answered. earth wind & fire *Open Our Eyes*. *Gratitude* is the best album.

The Inquisitive Eater, 2019

Silhouettes Aligned iii.

get yo money black man. My great great grandfather owned three farms and loved three wives. His wives were loving to each other, the farms, my granddaddy, and all 32 (?) children. We continue to discover more of our story, but most impeccable is this untethered bond that has bred four generations of black. children raised by three black women and their father a black man tending to farms and family on black owned southern land. sow hoe reap repeat. it seems he lived black in the American dream. tide was the only matter earth's axis had to manage all collateral damage pending the deconstruction of the black man.

car ride lullaby

Sleepless the night before
Labor Day weekend the cousins reunite
You know yo Family big when yall gotta have a reunion
just for the cousins. I live out dreams and daydreams until we arrive

The women crowd the kitchen: ribs, coconut shrimp, mac & cheese,
seafood salad, collard greens, corn on the cob, hot dogs, burgers,
and above all things sacred, my great grandmother's potato salad.
Meanwhile the men move to the wharf for some live crabs.

the smell of grass, charcoal, and old bay outback,
out front a street race
sunlight bouncing off dark backs
stretched arms and legs at the finish line

my great grandparents sit on the rocking bench beside my great
great aunt and uncle catching shade on Aunt Brenda's front porch.
the grass between my toes has drifted to the bottom of the inflatable pool.
popsicles and watermelon. pound cake and cherry pie.

the smell of outside inside
the flies never seem to find their way back outside
the feeling of being safe on the street. catching sunset and fireflies.
the smell of black and mild's, beer, weed and wine. cigarettes and raspy conversations,

line dances and hand games, songs guaranteed: September by Earth, Wind, & Fire,
Chuck Brown's Block Party, Love & Happiness by Al Green, Before I Let You
Go by Frankie Beverly & Maze. soft humming the smell of green Palmolive in
the kitchen we drift into the crevices of three houses, nearby motel rooms. B.E.T
cinema, Disney Channel movies, raunchy music videos, and quality bootlegs

                                              Sunday Breakfast Spot: Tommy's.
                        My Grandpa's name is Tom. To my cousin, he is Uncle Tom.
                          He is from Mississippi, fought in Nam and despises crackers.

packed compact cars and minivans, small cousins sit happily on top of big cousins,
grits, sausage, Belgium waffles, bacon, orange juice, forks and knives clanking
full mouths with bubbles on each side the table smiles full stomachs
chatter and laughter the stickiness of syrup between fingers cash only.

the waitress takes our family photo filled with chocolate, caramel, molasses, & cinnamon tones. long hugs and longer goodbyes before I am daydreaming out the window and the seatbelt is my pillow for the gentle car ride lullaby.

only time we heard dad curse

someone from the neighborhood shot a dog
& tossed this death over our fence.
a summoning as fresh as the carcass
abandoned wide mouthed grass-fed

words wounded and unintended for our ears, nonetheless
echoed, bobbed backyards, weaved alley ways leaving
a muffled message at our mistaken address. I wonder
if the owners would have reacted with a siren or stunned

or stunned silent had the message been delivered to its rightful owners
instead of my sister and I learning that dad could own anything profane.

Silhouettes Aligned

A black boy from the city trots to the riding lawn mower on his mother's southern acres. Meanwhile, she hangs sheets and towels on the line. Her grandchildren gather clothes to fold. She gathers the women for the commissary. The men gather at the wharf while that city boy rides that lawn mower across the street to his aunt's acres. After his first trip to the wharf with the men, a crab leaves the barrel and attaches itself to his nephew's boot. Laughter becomes baritone for his one footed prance.

The Explosion

the hero's wife:
"channel 7 got my name wrong. channel 5 got his name wrong.
channel 4 is the only news station with a good interview. the only one"

National Day of Prayer, May 7, 2009
a Thursday morning summer brings

gas bubbles above
between & beneath concrete

at Penn Marr Shopping Center in Forestville, Maryland
natural gas leaks seductively summer kisses
just before they touch their peak

eight firefighters are at the scene
evacuating 45 employees &
displeased customers see

what appears to be the source
of a bubbling pool of natural gas.
The fire captain who survived

the blast: "All I felt was heat
when I got to the rear
I glanced around the corner

the electric meter was on fire.
two choices go forward or go backward
I decided to close my eyes & dive

forward" flying bricks
dancing glass & blaze
ascending bright as lava

soaked in smoke fumes
rise beyond ceilings. clouds
sounding like calm before

the fire. the sound of a bomb.
the captain the hero, my father.
the hero's wife my mom:

"According to news your dad received
first & second degree burns on his hands & face,
but otherwise escaped unscathed
he managed to take off his wedding ring right before" it slumped into skin

for eternity eight firefighters one gas employee injured.
strip mall accident ends launch reconstruction
nearing the 1st anniversary of the explosion

dad retired from Prince George's County Fire Department:
"the past doesn't matter too much now. I must look forward."
even when the ground lifts the back roof & front become

disjointed still as peace
he dives forward.

Silhouettes Aligned ii.

"After he is stripped and castrated,
Claude Neal is forced to eat his own penis and testicles
as the angry mob of White women, men, and children applaud;
he is then forced to exclaim that he likes this physical
mutilation proves slight in comparison to the psychological
angst which inflicts Black men daily as they watch
their mothers, wives, and sisters raped.
Stripped and castrated they stood

powerless to this overt removal of authority within
a Family created despondency and disorder in the Black
man tainted by the constant swallowing of his manhood"[1]
This excerpt from A. Cooley's article *The Legacy of Lynching* is compost
for Kara Walker's fertile artwork in The New School's Arnhold Hall
Event Horizon covers corners and crannies along the main staircase
silhouettes reveal that color is less important than posture.
Some prance others free fall. Shoes appear selectively

so slaves, mistresses and masters can be easily recognized
for the people in the back the artwork chants, *'this is America'*.

a dream from New York to Detroit

I remember seeing mom intubated
before I knew what intubated meant.

I flew from New York to Detroit fast
asleep before takeoff, mild turbulence.

I see my mom in her casket.
I awaken.

I am in route to the double funeral
for her mother and sister.

dazed. its days after my college graduation,
which I don't remember

fainting after seeing my mom intubated
I know what intubated means now

we both lay in hospital beds
I squirm into fetal into my mom into consciousness

I remember waking up in the clouds gasping for air
encumbered by the seatbelt

sign sounds as faint as my heartbeat
my dream still stings.

within hours it was
inches from reality.

I remember duality.
I remember my first legal drink with my mom and sister

in the lobby of our Detroit hotel
days before the double funeral

for Aunt Melinda and Granma Daniels.
all three of us order a glass of wine.

before the drinks arrive,
my mother leaves the table.

my sister and I sit on discomfort and surprise
I see my dad's sober brown eyes.

he moves his mouth but there are no words.
his arms reach toward me. I stand
dazed, I hadn't eaten much today.
I don't remember these seconds

I remember these sounds.
silence, sirens, and my mom fighting to breathe

deep sigh deeper wheeze lungs pale
like mom's skin after they removed all the cancer,

which returned just one month before her sister passed
two months before her mother passed, three months before

my college graduation I don't remember, but I do
remember mistaking a cloudy premonition for a dream.

my world

I began sowing young.

I had seen so many die
suddenly, slowly, miraculously
I began to understand the value
of a life and a life unfulfilled.

dozens of funerals, wakes, repasses,
phone calls, news reports, social media
posts I keep trying to count how many
people I have known to live and then

die, so dad and I can
think back, do the math
to figure out how old I was
always wondering *who's next?*

all that to mean I invest in me
more than any other me that may be
reflecting from you. I invest in me
because I am whole.

a globe center begets a circle begets flattened rebirth:
straight lines beget four right angles
connecting squares
to mirrored triangles

whose world is this
it's mine it's mine it's mine.

Silhouettes Aligned iv.

A comedian discloses her unrelenting attraction to black men, though her options are limited. "It's nearly impossible to find a good black man. They're either married, got too many baby mamas, up under their momma, up under other women or men, under house arrest or incarcerated"...
Heard it all before. I got one more.
Nearly every elder has warned me about dating men close to my complexion, or with the last name Gaskins, or with family in South Carolina or D.C., or with the first name Robert, Reggie, or James (our tradition of recycling names). "You gotta know who they people are" I learned early that these precautions were necessary because of the three tribes
　　　　—I am a descendant of my great great grandfather's third wife.

Civil Eyes

a partial pantoum for the broken

you thought English was broken
blame adorned on aliens

captive generations that mother
while other vessels transport dis-ease

bodies blame the adorned alien
captives adapting abstract tongue

rhythm vessels transport dis-eases
bodies running through their veins

while adapting abstract tongue
rhythm generations mother

with other running through their veins
while captors trot to the velvet confusion

we were
fed
English

naturally
we chewed
English

teeny bites
we chew
English
to trans-mute
thoughts
choke

English
swallows
you
thought
English was broken
because it is
under attack
by ancestral aliens & rhythmic captives.

line leader

His story is linear like the schools
teach. Children long to be line leaders
while pipeline leaders prime for prison
stretching students from lines to sentences.

He masters the art. We are his pieces:
fragments of body & bone & blood
souls searching for home & land & Creator
& whole self-thrice-removed from Him

thorough bred in sin
he distorts light from within
his darkness his pale pink
ligaments blue green

rising against cold veins.
frigid is his hoodoo is his law
and his lightning strikes us:
sons of the sun we are his monster & muse. He soothes:

> *No one else will breathe*
> *our air. Fight against us*
> *if you dare, you of darker*
> *skin & coarser hair.*

guns

welcome
to the home of the big 3
Regur, Remington, and of course Smith & Wesson.
For decades they have been featured in your homes, on your televisions,
the highlight of your childhood arcade and video games,
inspiring some of the greatest music to date.
They reside at your local McDonald's, Wal-Mart
maybe even your grandmother's purse.
dependable, destructive, damned,
damn near, patriotic. now
occupying safer spaces:

Sandy Hook Elementary School, P.S. 202 Ernest S Jenkyns
Columbine High School Stoneman Douglass High School,
Red Lake High School… red lakes at 16th Street Baptist Church, Emanuael
African Methodist Episcopal Church, Christchurch of New Zealand,
Eastern Hills Elementary School, University of North Carolina, William C.
Longstreth Elementary School

now entering many young
hands triggered to invade

young bodies
young minds
young fear
young fearless

inside the dream institution

a tingly sensation before
poems begin in semesters
when I grip my pen with
calluses & dead skin cells

cracking confinement, divine
'alignment' moisturizes the
designed assignment climate
cricketed clocked critiques

cocky uncertain meek flocks
of sheep atop a hill, mean
while I'm flirting with the wind
thrusts evening twos & fours

years become keys keys open doors
now boomerang I seem to be flying
over yonder, grounded I speak to
the streets I am questioning the man

I fall into nudes for no one to taste
the proof burning crosses white
151 rum christens wood & skin
split by wind, thrusted & caught

by dream catchers worshipping ink
I am black birthed by the sphinx.

the dream institution

we sell dreams to the living
& lies to the giving folks
willing to invest in us
supple breasts force-feeding

bastards breeding Bachelors
& mothers breeding Masters
hold the bars of this cradle.

we'll burp you bathe you in a tub of
bubbly trust funded by eye crust &
dedication. we sell dreams to blinkers
& thinkers who believe prestigious 'schools' birthed education.

t•his•tory

> *Pledge allegiance to fight*
> *until the flag is torn;*
> *to chasing prominence*
> *until we cease to be*
> *born. Boys, to pilfer*
> *& murder lawfully*
> *you need a uniform;*
> *police, soldiers & heroes*

                    conform
        using law to breathe
         life into his story.
Books compress you until

      you become a caricature
        he concocts new poisons
to(o) paralyze(d) your ancestors
     become foggy fantasies now.

his story is linear
like the schools teach.

it's magic
how he & his father make me
disappear made you
disappear.

patriarchs, patriots, politicians
despise crime & envy competition

sustained dependency on supremacy
his debt his soul duty

s(he) with the PhD

there you be
with your PhD
Kanye told we: 'always had a Ph.D., *Pretty huge* …
well basically: 3 extra letters to 3 extra inches

3 more reasons why you're better than your nemesis
1. you could afford
2. you have a certificate to ignore things (like 4)
3. you have wealth without knowledge now you need knowledge no more

learning is for losers learning is 4
squares with no cash
girls with no ass
boys with no dad

all who don't hold the 3 letters you have/3 inches you brag.

civilized art

you say you're an artist, so you must know
what it means to use your hands
to shape a world between
mine and your own

fingertips collect
fibers
ink
prints
paintings
body movement
music
dance

muses that soothe when you inhale
whispers create carbon that shouts.
muses that heal moments that steal time
after time after time after day light jumps over the moon

a rounded ripple effect like double dutch
a roundish ripple effect like waves
a round ass ripple effect like days
after days of breathing in one world
while creating another
state of being
whole unfolded
still creased

                              you say you're an artist
                        but are you willing to sacrifice?
                                            to search
                                        to stand still

                                to buffer
                  to build up self, stick by stick
                  to discover destruction and decide
                                to suffer

                              suffer says the world
                                       suffer
                                   I'm suffering
                              sun down wind chimes

                                    still suffering
                  why do dollars stay coming on CP time?
                         why do I suffer line after line?
                    gaht dammit, I suffer every damn time

if you really are suffering you might not catch
these lines suffering very well may dwell in your mind
whereas for me, an artist,
suffering only lives in these stanzas

                                I align time after time,
                  whether in rhyme or with a quote to climb
                              I quilt quotients with words
                       from the colonizers who control minds

                                     uncertain unearthed,
worlds collide

guns grab

all that is
not growing
is dead.

children are
expecting to grow,
to stray
bullets designed to expand

puncture skin pierce organs
archive arteries and deflect bone.

                                        the exit
                                        wound
                                        invades
                                            an

                                                                             unpredictable
                                                                               farewell.

in the ancestral palm

aunt mary
her smile lines smooth skin
mahogany eyes crescent
moon mothering sky

great grandaddy
wide thighs made his lap
like the sofa without the
loud plastic covers

big mama
petite spicy sweet
big meaning matriarch of
our whole
Family

uncle George
strong and mighty voice
his cane merely a prop/lived
to be one hundred

and three with a sharp
mind/whole praying man/you must
know God for yourself

puddin
a gentle fragrance
fragile hands hold fragile me
her great granddaughter.

aunt melinda
my mother's sister.
nine years separated them,
but her hugs warmed me.

granpa dortch
my god father/I
remember tying his shoe
in the living room.

large dark hands that bent
at the knuckles/he fixed cars
with my father/my

dad's adopted dad
was my god father/though I
still called him granpa.

adeyinke cynthia
if it isn't nice
and necessary, it does
not need to be said.

aunt monique
present at Christmas
she died before New Year's Eve.
gradually, we grieve.

uncle reggie
I'd get lost in his
hugs/the bass from his guitar
found in my tummy

uncle james
hugs and wet kisses
cigarettes and silky grey
hair in eight straight backs

raspy but smooth voice
smoother walk/respected by
the church family hood

granma jesse
fresh manicure/helped
raise the neighborhood children
and four of her own

ms. battles
I remember her
stories, songs, laugh/my treasured
teacher could have been

my aunt/sister friend
to mom/but she died too soon
so I imagine

nina gaskin
fly gator boots/church
hats colorful/loved you with
the love of the Lord

if I remember
correctly, wanted me with
one of her grandsons

ed gaskin
tamed tenor/dreamy
alto/church choir solos
transitioned too soon

ACKNOWLEDGMENTS

All that you touch
you change.
All that you change
changes you.
The only lasting truth
is change.
God is change.

-OCTAVIA BUTLER

C&R PRESS CHAPBOOKS

C&R Press hosts two chapbook selection periods from June to September and November to March coupled with a reading in New York City each year. The Winter Soup Bowl and Summer Tide Pool Chapbook Series are open to new and established writers in poetry, fiction, essay and other creative writing.

2019 Summer Tide Pool
The Magical Negro Reveals His Secret by Gabriel Green

2018 Winter Soup Bowl
Paleotemptestology by Bertha Crombet
White Boys from Hell by Jeffrey Skinner

2017 Summer Tide Pool
Atypical Cells of Undetermined Significance by Brenna Womer

2017 Winter Soup Bowl
Heredity and Other Inventions by Sharona Muir
On Inaccuracy by Joe Manning

2016 Summer Tide Pool
Cuntstruck by Kate Northrop
Relief Map by Erin M. Bertram
Love Undefined by Jonathan Katz

2016 Winter Soup Bowl
Notes from the Negro Side of the Moon by Earl Braggs
A Hunger Called Music: A Verse History in Black Music by Meredith Nnoka

C&R PRESS TITLES

NONFICTION

Women in the Literary Landscape by Doris Weatherford, et al
Credo: An Anthology of Writing Manifestos by Rita Banerjee and Diana Norma Szokolyai

FICTION

Last Tower to Heaven by Jacob Paul
No Good, Very Bad Asian by Lelund Cheuk
Surrendering Appomattox by Jacob M. Appel
Made by Mary by Laura Catherine Brown
Ivy vs. Dogg by Brian Leung
While You Were Gone by Sybil Baker
Cloud Diary by Steve Mitchell
Spectrum by Martin Ott
That Man in Our Lives by Xu Xi

SHORT FICTION

Two Californias by Robert Glick
Notes From the Mother Tongue by An Tran
The Protester Has Been Released by Janet Sarbanes

ESSAY AND CREATIVE NONFICTION

In the Room of Persistent Sorry by Kristina Marie Darling
the internet is for real by Chris Campanioni
Immigration Essays by Sybil Baker
Je suis l'autre: Essays and Interrogations by Kristina Marie Darling
Death of Art by Chris Campanioni

POETRY

What Need Have We for Such as We by Amanda Auerbach
A Family Is a House by Dustin Pearson
The Miracles by Amy Lemmon
Banjo's Inside Coyote by Kelli Allen
Objects in Motion by Jonathan Katz
My Stunt Double by Travis Denton
Lessons in Camoflauge by Martin Ott
Millennial Roost by Dustin Pearson
Dark Horse by Kristina Marie Darling
All My Heroes are Broke by Ariel Francisco
Holdfast by Christian Anton Gerard
Ex Domestica by E.G. Cunningham
Like Lesser Gods by Bruce McEver
Negro Side of the Moon by Earl Braggs
Imagine Not Drowning by Kelli Allen
Notes to the Beloved by Michelle Bitting
Free Boat: Collected Lies and Love Poems by John Reed
Les Fauves by Barbara Crooker
Tall as You are Tall Between Them by Annie Christain
The Couple Who Fell to Earth by Michelle Bitting

www.ingramcontent.com/pod-product-compliance
Lightning Source LLC
Chambersburg PA
CBHW032106040426
42449CB00007B/1209